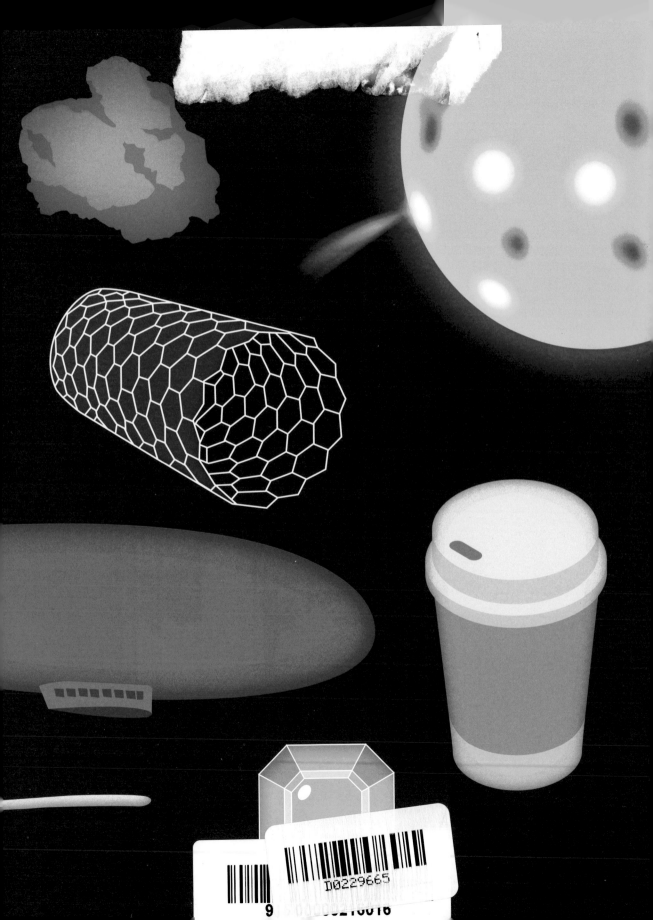

First published in Great Britain
in 2019 by Wayland
Copyright © Hodder and Stoughton, 2019
All rights reserved

Editor: Amy Pimperton
Text written by Rob Colson and
Jon Richards
Produced by Tall Tree Ltd
Designers: Malcolm Parchment and
Ben Ruocco

HB ISBN: 978 1 5263 0780 4
PB ISBN: 978 1 5263 0781 1

Wayland
An imprint of Hachette Children's Group
Part of Hodder and Stoughton
Carmelite House
50 Victoria Embankment
London EC4Y 0DZ

An Hachette UK Company
www.hachette.co.uk
www.hachettechildrens.co.uk

Printed in China

MIX
Paper from
responsible sources
FSC® C104740
FSC
www.fsc.org

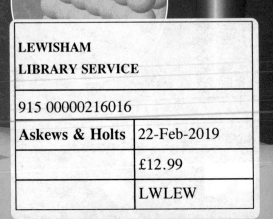

MATERIALS AND MATTER

Everything around you is made up from tiny particles called atoms. How these atoms behave and interact with each other defines what type of matter an object is made from.

STATES OF MATTER

There are **three** main types, or states, of matter:

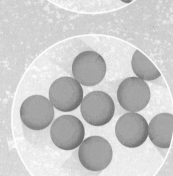

Solid: A solid has its atoms arranged in a closely packed structure. Its volume and shape are fixed.

Liquid: The atoms in a liquid are loosely attracted to each other. A liquid can flow and, while its volume won't change, it will take on the shape of the container holding it.

Gas: The atoms in a gas aren't attracted to each other and a gas will expand to fill any container holding it.

THICK LIQUID

Some liquids are so thick that they appear to be solid. In an experiment in Queensland, Australia, a blob of thick pitch has been dripping through a funnel since 1927. Large drops fall at a rate of one drop per decade. That makes pitch about 230 billion times thicker than water.

A FOURTH STATE

Many scientists say that there is a fourth state of matter – **plasma**. This is a hot mixture of positively and negatively charged particles that can conduct electricity. Examples include stars such as our Sun, aurorae and bolts of lightning. Most of the matter in the Universe is plasma.

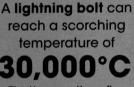

Stars are huge burning balls of plasma.

A bolt of lightning is a sudden flow of electric charge along a narrow channel of plasma.

A **lightning bolt** can reach a scorching temperature of

30,000°C

That's more than five times hotter than the surface of the Sun!

5

PROPERTIES

Scientists define different materials and types of matter by the properties they have.

Thermal properties: These can include a substance's melting point or boiling point.

Physical properties: These can include the strength, hardness, mass and elasticity of a substance.

Atomic properties: These are the mass, weight and atomic number of the tiny atoms that make up the substance.

CARBON

Diamonds and coal are made from the same element – **carbon**. However, they have very different properties because their atoms are arranged differently. Diamonds are extremely hard and very difficult to burn. Coal is softer and burns easily.

Coal is burned to make heat.

Diamonds have a rough shape that can be cut and polished to make jewellery.

ATOMIC BUILDING BLOCKS

All matter, whether solid, liquid, gas or plasma, is made up of particles called atoms. But even these tiny objects are made from smaller and smaller objects, and scientists need some of the biggest machines ever built to study them.

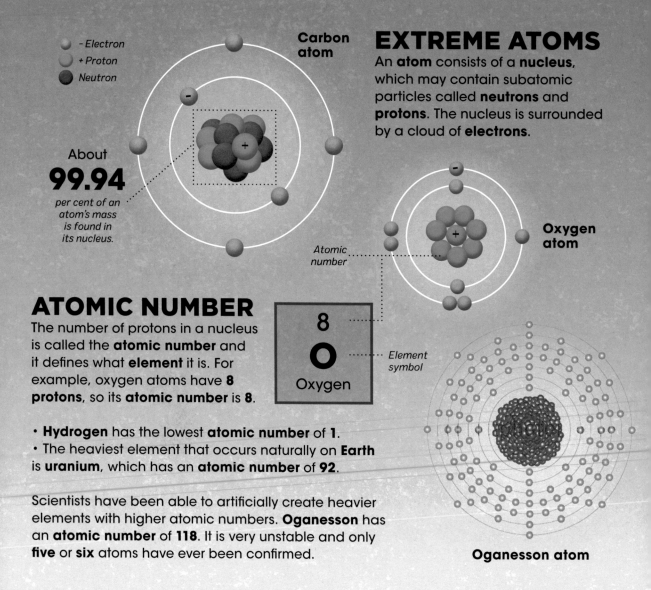

- Electron
+ Proton
Neutron

Carbon atom

About
99.94
per cent of an atom's mass is found in its nucleus.

EXTREME ATOMS

An **atom** consists of a **nucleus**, which may contain subatomic particles called **neutrons** and **protons**. The nucleus is surrounded by a cloud of **electrons**.

Oxygen atom

Atomic number

8
O
Oxygen

Element symbol

ATOMIC NUMBER

The number of protons in a nucleus is called the **atomic number** and it defines what **element** it is. For example, oxygen atoms have **8 protons**, so its **atomic number** is **8**.

- **Hydrogen** has the lowest **atomic number** of **1**.
- The heaviest element that occurs naturally on **Earth** is **uranium**, which has an **atomic number** of **92**.

Scientists have been able to artificially create heavier elements with higher atomic numbers. **Oganesson** has an **atomic number** of **118**. It is very unstable and only **five** or **six** atoms have ever been confirmed.

Oganesson atom

SUPERSTAR SQUEEZER

If temperatures and pressures are high enough, atomic nuclei can be squeezed together to fuse and make heavier elements. For example, in the core of a star, such as our Sun, hydrogen nuclei are fused together to make heavier helium nuclei. This releases lots of energy, causing the star to shine.

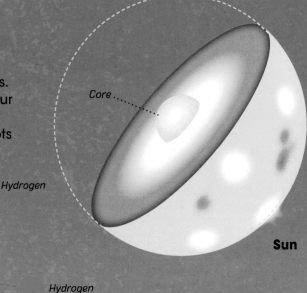

Core

Sun

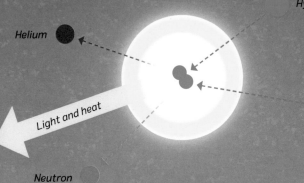

Hydrogen

Helium

Light and heat

Hydrogen

Neutron

In the LHC, atoms smash into one another at nearly the speed of light.

ATOM SMASHER

The **Large Hadron Collider** (LHC) at the research institute **CERN** is one of the biggest machines ever built. It consists of a **27-kilometre** ring and powerful super-conducting magnets that hurl atoms at incredible speeds so that they smash into each other. This creates even smaller subatomic particles, which scientists hope will reveal more about the secrets of the Universe and how it functions.

Building the Large Hadron Collider involved more than

10,000

scientists from over 100 countries.

BOILING AND CONDENSING

Whether a substance is a gas, solid or liquid depends on the energy levels of its atoms – change the energy levels and the substance may move from one state to another.

FROM LIQUID TO GAS

Increasing the energy levels of the atoms in a substance will cause them to vibrate more energetically. Give them enough energy and the bonds between them will break, causing them to change state. Changing from a liquid to a gas is called boiling.

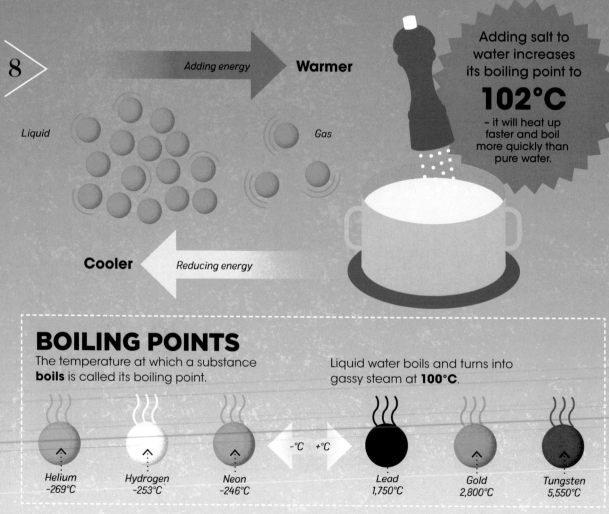

Adding energy

Warmer

Liquid

Gas

Adding salt to water increases its boiling point to

102°C

– it will heat up faster and boil more quickly than pure water.

Cooler

Reducing energy

BOILING POINTS

The temperature at which a substance **boils** is called its boiling point.

Liquid water boils and turns into gassy steam at **100°C**.

-°C   +°C

Helium	Hydrogen	Neon	Lead	Gold	Tungsten
-269°C	-253°C	-246°C	1,750°C	2,800°C	5,550°C

BOILING AND PRESSURE

Boiling points are affected by pressure. Water boils at **100°C** at **sea level**. At the top of **Mount Everest**, where air pressure is lower, water boils at just **69°C**. The water gushing out of **hydrothermal vents** deep on the ocean floor can reach more than **450°C**, but because of the high pressure at these depths it remains as a liquid.

Super-heated water gushes out of deep hydrothermal vents

EVAPORATION

Water doesn't always need to boil to turn into a gas. Some molecules at the water's surface may have enough energy to break the bonds holding them together and escape – this is called evaporation. Boiling happens throughout a liquid, but evaporation can only happen at the surface.

MELTING AND FREEZING

Reducing the amount of energy of a substance's atoms can also change its state. For example, freezing a substance changes it from a liquid into a solid.

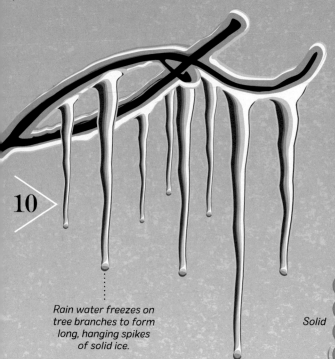

Rain water freezes on tree branches to form long, hanging spikes of solid ice.

FROM **SOLID** TO **LIQUID**

Adding energy or heat to a solid makes its particles vibrate more energetically. Add enough heat and the bonds between the particles break down and the particles start to flow, forming a liquid. **Reduce the energy** of the particles in a liquid by cooling it enough and bonds between the particles will form, causing the liquid to freeze into a solid.

Adding energy → **Warmer**

Liquid

Solid

Cooler ← Reducing energy

MELTING POINTS

Water melts at **0°C**. Other substances have much higher or lower melting points.

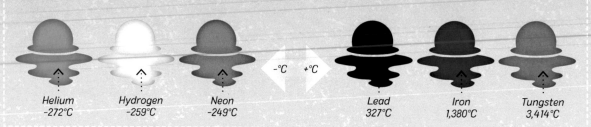

Helium	Hydrogen	Neon			Lead	Iron	Tungsten
-272°C	-259°C	-249°C	-°C +°C		327°C	1,380°C	3,414°C

MELTING AND FREEZING POINTS

Most substances melt into a liquid or freeze into a solid at the same temperature. **Agar** is an unusual substance that has different melting and freezing points. It turns from a solid into a liquid at **85°C**, but turns from a liquid into a solid at just **32°C**.

Some living things can survive long periods at sub-freezing temperatures. One species of **nematode** worm was found to survive being frozen for more than **44 weeks** at temperatures of nearly

-200°C

SUBLIMATION

Sublimation occurs when a solid turns into a gas without becoming a liquid. **Solid carbon dioxide** is known as **dry ice**. It turns into a gas at room temperature, and is used to create smoke effects on stage.

FLOATING ICE

Most substances reduce in volume when they freeze into a solid, including water actually expand. This is why ice cubes float in a drink and icebergs float in the ocean.

SOFTEST AND HARDEST

Many scientists use the Mohs scale to define the hardness of different minerals. It rates minerals on a scale of one to ten, with one for the softest and ten for the hardest.

FROM SOFT TO HARD

The Mohs scale grades hardness by comparing how minerals can scratch other minerals. The scale was created in 1812 by the German geologist Friedrich Mohs (1773–1839), but his method for grading materials by comparing scratches is thousands of years old, and was used by the ancient Greeks and Romans.

PENCIL LEAD

Graphite is a very soft form of carbon. It is made up of thin sheets of carbon atoms that slide easily over each other.

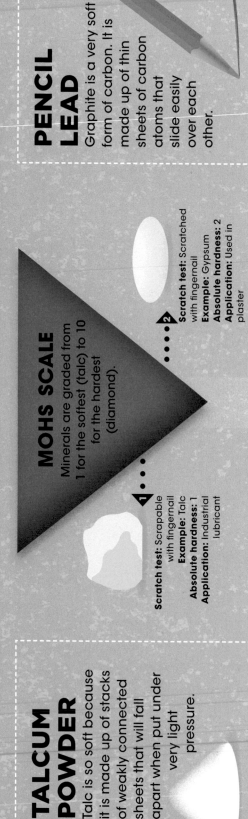

MOHS SCALE

Minerals are graded from 1 for the softest (talc) to 10 for the hardest (diamond).

1

Scratch test: Scrapable with fingernail
Example: Talc
Absolute hardness: 1
Application: Industrial lubricant

2

Scratch test: Scratched with fingernail
Example: Gypsum
Absolute hardness: 2
Application: Used in plaster

TALCUM POWDER

Talc is so soft because it is made up of stacks of weakly connected sheets that will fall apart when put under very light pressure.

HARDER THAN DIAMOND

Diamond is so hard because its carbon atoms are strongly bonded together in a regular pattern. It was thought that the only thing that could scratch diamond was another diamond. However, in 2009, scientists discovered that another rare mineral made of carbon, lonsdaleite, is 58 per cent harder than diamond.

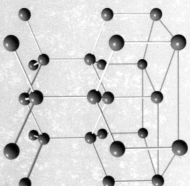

The carbon atoms in diamond and lonsdaleite are each bonded to three other atoms in a strong lattice. In lonsdaleite, these lattices are arranged in regular hexagonal layers.

ABSOLUTE HARDNESS

'Absolute hardness' is measured by an instrument called a **sclerometer**, which is used to compare how easily a material can be scratched by another.

Sclerometer

STRONG BONES

The hardest materials in your body are bone tissue, which is four times stronger than concrete, and the enamel that covers your teeth. Tooth enamel measures five on the Mohs scale, making it one of the hardest biological materials.

Bones contain a number of different minerals that make them hard, including crystals of calcium phosphate. Tooth enamel is made mostly of calcium phosphate, and is even harder than bone.

INCREASING HARDNESS

3
Scratch test: Scratched with a copper coin
Example: Calcite
Absolute hardness: 9
Application: Used in cement

4
Scratch test: Easily scratched with a nail
Example: Fluorite
Absolute hardness: 21
Application: Used in toothpaste

5
Scratch test: Scratched a little with a nail
Example: Apatite
Absolute hardness: 48
Application: Mineral in bone

6
Scratch test: Scratched with a steel file
Example: Orthoclase
Absolute hardness: 72
Application: Used in glass

7
Scratch test: Scratches glass
Example: Quartz
Absolute hardness: 100
Application: Building material

8
Scratch test: Scratches quartz
Example: Topaz
Absolute hardness: 200
Application: Gemstone

9
Scratch test: Scratches topaz
Example: Corundum
Absolute hardness: 400
Application: Gemstone

10
Scratch test: Scratches corundum
Example: Diamond
Absolute hardness: 1,500
Application: Industrial drills

GETTING HEAVY

These materials are some of the densest, heaviest and most massive on the planet ... and beyond! You may need something a little stronger than a wheelbarrow to move these substances around!

HEAVY METAL

Some of the densest materials on Earth are a group of elements called heavy metals. All of these would sink very quickly in water, which weighs 1 g/cm³.

ELEMENT	WEIGHT
Lead	11.3 g/cm³
Mercury (densest liquid)	13.5 g/cm³
Gold	19.32 g/cm³
Platinum	21.46 g/cm³
Iridium	22.56 g/cm³
Osmium	22.6 g/cm³

HEAVY WEIGHT

Osmium is the heaviest naturally occurring element on Earth.

A mixture of **OSMIUM** and **IRIDIUM** is used to make the nibs for fountain pens.

Nib is made of a durable metal alloy.

GOLD BARS

Gold is commonly bought and sold in bars weighing 1 kg. The bars are just 8 cm long, 4 cm wide and 2 cm thick – the size of a small chocolate bar. They weigh the same as a one-litre bottle of water.

This small gold bar weighs the same as a litre of water.

8 cm

BEYOND EARTH

Beyond Earth (and even the Solar System) things can become very extreme.

Neutron stars are the super dense remains of stars that exploded in a supernova. They may only be about 10 km across, but they can have twice the mass of the Sun. A thimble-full of matter from a neutron star would weigh as much as 12 million elephants.

Each elephant equals one million

BLACK HOLES

Black holes are the densest objects in the Universe. They are formed when very massive stars explode in a supernova, leaving behind a region of space that is so dense and has such a strong gravitational field that nothing can escape it – not even light!

A black hole sucks in matter and light. Nothing can cross the event horizon from inside the black hole.

Event horizon

Black hole

LIGHTER THAN A FEATHER

These incredible materials have been used to carry people high into the air from more than 100 years and may also prove extremely helpful in the future of building and transport technology.

INTO THE AIR

The lightest elements in the Universe are **hydrogen** and **helium**, both of which are lighter than air and can be used to lift airships off the ground.

Hydrogen has a density about $\frac{1}{14}$**th** that of air.

The lifting gas in an airship is contained in one or more internal gas bags or cells.

Aerogels have many applications, including thermal insulation and electronics.

AEROGELS

Silica aerogels are **99.8** per cent air. They are made from gels that have had their liquid parts replaced with gas, creating a material so light that it has been dubbed '**solid air**'. It has a density of **1,000 g/m³**. By comparison, the density of air is 1,200 g/m³.

OUT OF THIS WORLD

Silica aerogel's heat-retaining properties make it the perfect material for use as insulation in space, where it is used in the lining of **spacesuits** and as a protective coating for the **Mars Rovers**. It has also been used to make lightweight space probes to trap and return **space dust** to Earth.

Space is very, very .... cold – roughly 2.7 Kelvin (–270.45°C), so spacesuits need to be very well insulated.

AEROGRAPHITE

Aerographite is an artificial foam made from a network of tiny carbon tubes. It has a density of just **180 g/m³**.

AEROGRAPHENE

Aerographene is the solid with the **lowest density of all**. It consists of an exterior that's made from graphene supported by an interior of carbon nanotubes. It has a density of just **160 g/m³**, which is **lighter than helium** and **7.5 times less dense than air**. This incredible substance is extremely porous and can soak up 900 times its own weight in oil, which means it could be very useful in mopping up polluting oil spills.

Aerographene fills .... with air, making it so light that a large block of it can balance on even the most delicate blades of grass.

METALLIC MICROLATTICES

Metallic microlattices are a very light metal foam that are **99.99 per cent** air with a density of **2,100 g/m³**. They can be compressed a great deal and could be used to make shock absorbers to use in cars and planes and even spring-loaded energy storing devices.

RARE AND COMMON

Materials aren't spread evenly throughout Earth and the Universe and some substances are more common than others. Some of these materials are incredibly rare, while others are all around us in the air we breathe or the ground beneath our feet.

MOST COMMON

Hydrogen and **helium** are the most common elements. Hydrogen makes up **74 per cent** of the ordinary matter we can see and detect, while helium makes up **24 per cent**. But this ordinary matter forms just a tiny piece of the Universe – only about **5 per cent**. The rest is made up of **27 per cent** dark matter and **65 per cent** dark energy – but no-one knows exactly what these are.

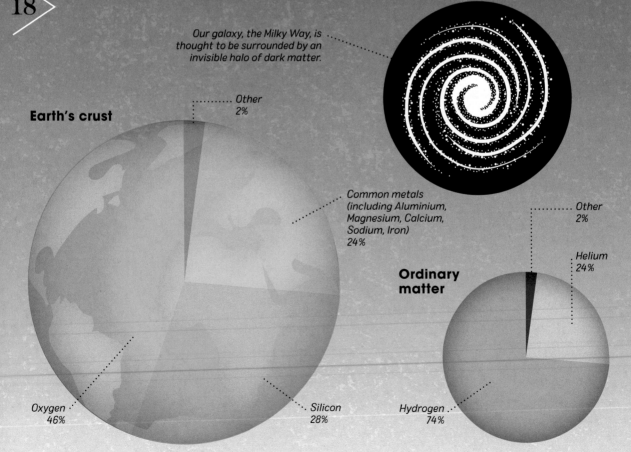

Our galaxy, the Milky Way, is thought to be surrounded by an invisible halo of dark matter.

Earth's crust

Other
2%

Common metals
(including Aluminium,
Magnesium, Calcium,
Sodium, Iron)
24%

Other
2%

Helium
24%

Ordinary matter

Oxygen
46%

Silicon
28%

Hydrogen
74%

ANTIMATTER

This is produced naturally by cosmic rays from outer space and above thunderstorms on Earth. Tiny amounts of this mysterious material have been produced artificially at an estimated cost of US**$25 billion per gram**.

CALIFORNIUM

This can only be produced artificially on Earth, but may be formed in the immense heat and pressure of a supernova. It is used to start nuclear reactors and costs about US**$18.7 million per gram**.

Californium was first made in a laboratory in California in 1950. **Californium is RADIOACTIVE.**

CHANCE DISCOVERY

This mauve gem is thought to be a million times scarcer than diamond. Having been previously misidentified as another gem, spinel, it was discovered by accident in a jewellers in Dublin, Ireland, in 1945. It is named **taaffeite** after Richard Taaffe (1898–1967), the gemmologist who discovered it.

RAREST MATERIALS

Astatine is said to be the rarest natural element on Earth. It's very unstable with a half-life (the time required for any specified property to decrease by half) of **8.1 hours** and there's only about **30 g** of it in Earth's crust (about the weight of five 10-pence coins). Just **0.05 micrograms** has been produced so far. Nobody has ever seen it because before you have enough to see, it is vaporised by its own radioactivity.

ELASTIC AND PLASTIC

Apply a force to a material and it may bend, stretch or even break. How it reacts to this force and how it behaves after the force has been removed defines how plastic or elastic a substance is.

ELASTIC

When a force is applied, it changes the shape of a material, but when the force is removed, the material returns to its original shape – this is called elastic deformation.

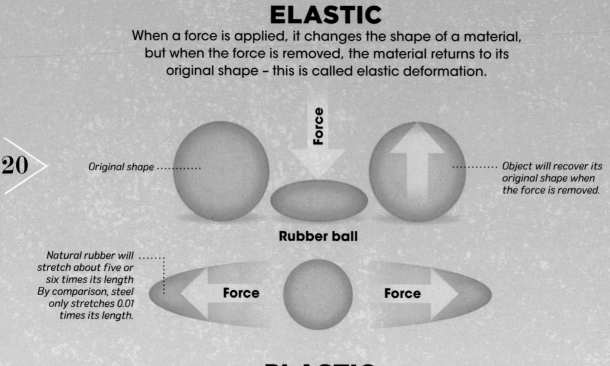

Force

Original shape ....

Object will recover its original shape when the force is removed.

Rubber ball

Natural rubber will stretch about five or six times its length By comparison, steel only stretches 0.01 times its length.

Force

Force

PLASTIC

When a force is applied, it changes the shape of a material, and when the force is removed, the material retains its new shape – this is called plastic deformation.

Original shape ....

Applying force or heat changes the shape of a material permanently.

Force

Plastic spoon

RUBBER TREES

Natural rubber is made from the **dried sap** of rubber trees. The sap is tapped from the trunks of the trees. The first recorded use of rubber was by the **Olmecs** in present-day Mexico 3,000 years ago. They played sport with a rubber ball.

Sap tap

Rubber sap

Sap catcher

HYDROGELS

Hydrogels are made from a network of chains of chemicals called **polymers** that are held in water. They are very elastic and can be stretched up to **20 times** their length and return to their original size. They are highly absorbent and can swell to contain as much as **90 per cent** water. This makes them ideal for **medical dressings** and nappies. In farming, hydrogels are used to water crops and to control the release of pesticides and fertilisers.

PLASTIC POLLUTION

Plastics are one of the most widely used materials on the planet. We have produced more plastic in the last **ten** years than in the previous **100** years. Plastic production uses about **8 per cent** of the world's **oil** production. Over time, plastics break down into tiny particles called **microplastics**. These end up in the oceans, where they are eaten by **marine creatures**, and are thought to cause extensive harm.

About **50%** of the plastic we make is used once and then thrown away.

Globally, **500 BILLION** plastic bags are used each year.

CONDUCTING AND INSULATING

Heat energy can move through materials by conduction. Some materials, such as metals, are good at conducting heat. Other materials can trap heat, making them insulators. Similarly, metals conduct the flow of electricity, while other materials resist electricity.

CONDUCTING HEAT

1. Energy from a heat source starts to warm part of a material.

2. As the material is heated, the atoms closest to the heat source start to vibrate more.

3. The vibrations are spread to neighbouring atoms, transferring the energy and the heat.

Cold Atoms

Heat

Atoms energised and vibration increases

Heat

Vibrations spread through other atoms

Heat

K-VALUE

Heat conduction is measured in units called watts per meter kelvin (**W/mK**), also known as the **k-value**. The higher a material's k-value, the more quickly it conducts heat.

BEST THERMAL CONDUCTORS

Element	k-value
Diamond	1,000
Copper	401
Aluminium	237

The bottoms of pans are often made from copper, which is an excellent heat conductor. This spreads the heat quickly and evenly across the pan.

WORST THERMAL CONDUCTORS

Element	k-value
Silica aerogel	0.02
Polyurethane foam	0.0201–0.021
Expanded polystyrene	0.033–0.046
Fibreglass or foam glass	0.045

These materials are good insulators. They are used to **keep objects warm** and can be found in **disposable cups** for hot drinks and **home insulation**.

The energy of the warm coffee molecules cannot easily pass through the cup's walls, so the drink stays hot for longer.

Gases are not good conductors because their **PARTICLES** are spread too far apart.

CONDUCTING ELECTRICITY

As well as conducting heat, metals also allow electricity to flow through them easily. Materials that stop electricity from flowing and are known as electrical insulators. Metals such as **copper** and **aluminium** make the best electrical conductors and copper is used to make electrical wires.

The best electrical insulators include plastic, wood, glass and rubber. **Plastics** are used to insulate electrical wires to stop electrical shocks.

Copper wire

Plastic cable jacket

Plastic insulation

SUPERCONDUCTORS

Superconductors are metals that have little or no electrical resistance at very low temperatures. This means that they can transmit power without losses, and can be used to make super-fast circuits, and amazingly powerful electromagnets.

FLOATING TRAINS

Maglev trains use magnets to keep them floating above the guide rails and power them along at incredible speeds. Their superconducting magnets are cooled using liquid helium.

Guide rail

Levitation magnets

Guide magnets

STRONGEST

Super strong and amazingly tough, materials don't get more resilient than these substances. Some are created in Earth's most violent events, while others are produced artificially in laboratories.

DIAMOND

A tough form of carbon that's used on the **tips of drills** and as **jewellery**. They form deep underground, where there are high pressures and temperatures.

Rough, uncut diamond

Polished, cut diamond

WURTZITE BORON NITRIDE

This naturally occurring substance is very rare. It only forms in the extreme heat and pressure of large **volcanic eruptions**. It is **18 per cent** harder than diamond.

Volcanic rock

Meteor

LONSDALEITE

An even rarer naturally occurring material as it's only formed when **meteors** slam into Earth. It's **58 per cent** harder than diamond.

Lava flow

SILICON CARBIDE

Also found in **meteorites** but also produced artificially, it's tougher than diamond and used in **tank armour**.

Also known as carborundum, it is a semiconductor containing silicon and carbon with the chemical formula

SiC

It occurs in nature as the extremely rare mineral moissanite.

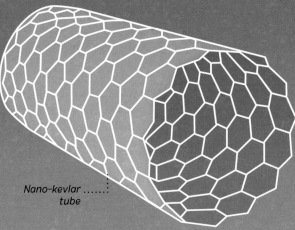

Nano-kevlar tube

NANO-KEVLAR

These **ultra-thin** tubes of the **bullet-proof** material are **100,000 times thinner** than a human hair and could be used in the future to produce artificial cartilage to repair damaged joints.

25

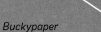

Buckypaper

GRAPHENE

Formed from atom-thick sheets of carbon, this material is **200 times stronger** than steel and can conduct electricity. It could be used to make **tough display screens**, **electrical circuits**, **solar cells**, as well as in a wide range of **medical**, **chemical** and industrial processes.

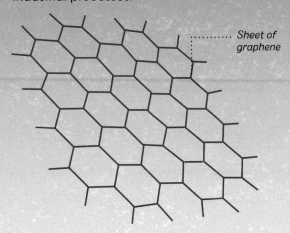

Sheet of graphene

BUCKYPAPER

A thin sheet made from **carbon nanotubes**, buckypaper is **50,000 times** thinner than a human hair but **500 times** stronger than steel and **10 times** lighter. In the future, it could be used to produce super-tough body and tank armour as well as cutting-edge electronics.

NATURAL WONDERS

Nature provides some of its own materials with super-extreme attributes, and we humans are trying to harness these properties for our uses.

SUPER-TOUGH SILK

Spiders produce a special type of protein fibre, called spider silk, which they weave to create webs, homes and traps. This thin thread has some amazing characteristics.

Spider silk is **five times** stronger than **steel** and can stretch up to five times its normal length without breaking.

Spiders use spider silk to:
- **Catch prey** – webs form food-catching nets.
- **Immobilise prey** – some spiders wrap prey in silk to stop it escaping.
- **Fly** – some spiders use threads of silk to catch the wind and fly from place to place.
- **Set trip wires** – some spiders lay out long lines of thread to warn them of approaching prey.

SUPER WEB

The silk of Darwin's bark spider, found in Madagascar, is the toughest of all – up to **ten times tougher** than **Kevlar**. The spider uses it to weave huge webs nearly 2 m across.

Spider silk

COPYING NATURE

Scientists are trying to copy the properties of spider silk to produce super-tough **ropes**, **nets**, **seat belts**, **parachutes** and **bullet-proof** clothing.

Parachute .... cords

Parachute canopy

FAST GRASS

Bamboo is the fastest-growing plant, growing at up to **90 cm** a day, or **0.00003 kph**, and to a height of **40 m**.

Strong wood fibres can resist a force of
5 kN/cm².

Steel can resist up to
37 kN/cm².

Bamboo tubes can resist up to
40 kN/cm².

Bamboo is an incredibly useful material that can be used to make paper, cloth and building materials. In some parts of the world, bamboo is used in scaffolding instead of steel tubes.

GET A GRIP!

Limpet teeth contain the **strongest biological material** ever tested.

• The shellfish use these teeth to grip tightly to rocks. It's been measured as **five times stronger** than spider silk. It is also stronger than Kevlar fibres and almost as good as carbon-fibre materials.

• The teeth are made from tiny nanofibres made from a mineral called **goethite** that is embedded in **chitin**.

• Scientists could stretch samples of this material to four times their original length without breaking.

..... Bamboo stem

COMBINING MATERIALS

If one substance doesn't perform well enough, then you can always try mixing two or more together. The resulting composite materials can be lightweight, easy to use and incredibly strong.

EARLY BUILDINGS

Some of the earliest building materials were composites. Mud and straw have been mixed together and baked to make bricks for more than **9,000 years**. Some of the earliest examples of these mud bricks have been found at **Mehrgarh** in what is now **Pakistan**.

Thatched roof

Mud and straw bricks

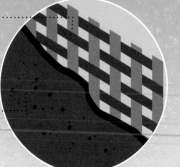

Strips of wood interwoven

Wet mud and straw spread over lattice structure

WATTLE AND DAUB

Wattle and daub features a **woven lattice** of wooden strips (the wattle) on to which **wet mud, clay, straw** and even **dung** (the daub) is spread to produce a wall once it's dried. It was first used more than **6,000 years ago**.

CONCRETE

Concrete is a mixture of **cement** (a fine powder made from limestone and clay) and an **aggregate**, such as **sand** or **gravel**. It is the most common artificial material with more than **7.5 billion cubic metres** made each year.

Concrete is usually

60–75%
Aggregate
(sand and gravel)

5–8%
Air

10–15%
Cement

15–20%
Water

PYKRETE

Pykrete is a mixture of **frozen water (86 per cent)** and **wood pulp (14 per cent)**. It is so strong that it is bulletproof, and it melts very slowly. During the Second World War (1939–45), a British proposal was put forward to create a huge **super-sized aircraft carrier** made from pykrete. Known as **Operation Habakkuk** it would have provided air cover for ship convoys across the Atlantic, but was abandoned due to rising costs and changing priorities.

Pykrete is slightly more difficult to form than concrete, as it **EXPANDS** during the freezing process.

Pykrete is made from wood (usually waste wood) chipped into a specific size.

CARBON FIBRE

Modern carbon fibre materials feature **small, thin fibres** of carbon that are set in a **matrix** within a resin. Carbon fibre is used to make **lightweight** and **strong** vehicle parts and to **reinforce** existing structures.

Carbon strand

Resin

GLOSSARY

ARTIFICIAL
Something that is man-made, like a machine, rather than occurring naturally in the environment.

ATOM
Tiny particles that are the building blocks of all matter. Atoms combine to form molecules.

ATOMIC NUCLEUS
The small, dense region at the centre of an atom. It contains nearly all of the atom's mass.

AURORA
A colourful natural light display that occurs at night in the Northern and Southern hemispheres.

CHITIN
A chemical that is the main ingredient in the shells of arthropods, such as insects, and in the shells of molluscs such as limpets.

COSMIC RAYS
Highly energetic particles from outside the solar system that travel through space at very high speeds.

DENSITY
The measure of how tightly packed molecules are within an object. High-density objects have more tightly packed molecules.

ELASTICITY
The measure of how able an object or material is to return to its original shape after being squashed or stretched.

EVENT HORIZON
The boundary around the mouth of a black hole. Past this point, nothing can escape being sucked in – even light.

FERTILISER
A substance that is used to make plants and crops grow better, often made of animal manure or nitrates.

FORCE
Can cause an object to speed up, slow down, stay still or change shape by exerting a push or a pull.

INSULATION
A material or substance used to block or reduce the amount of heat, sound or electricity that can pass through it.

MAGNET
Often made of a metal such as iron or steel, a magnet attracts other magnetic materials towards it. Magnets have a north and south pole, and a magnetic field.

MASS
The amount of matter that an object contains.

METEORITE
Chunks of rock that fall from space, survive the atmosphere, and reach Earth's surface without burning up.

MINERAL
Found on Earth's surface as well as deep underground, minerals make up sand, soil and rocks.

NEUTRON STAR
Created when a giant star dies in a supernova and its core collapses in on itself. They are small but extremely dense.

PESTICIDE
A chemical substance that is used to kill insects and weeds thought of as pests.

PITCH
The name given to a thick, black substance that is sometimes painted on to boats and houses to make them waterproof.

PRESSURE
The measure of weight or force exerted on a surface. The amount of pressure decreases as surface area increases.

PROTON
A particle with positive electrical charge, found inside atoms.

RADIOACTIVE
Materials that are radioactive give out radiation in the form of waves or particles. Radiation can be dangerous or useful, depending on its properties.

SOLAR CELLS
Devices that convert light energy from the Sun into usable electrical energy. Solar power is renewable because it doesn't run out.

SPACE DUST
Made up of very small particles of matter that can be found right across the known Universe. Also known as cosmic dust.

SPACESUIT
Specially-designed clothing that protects an astronaut from extreme temperatures, lack of oxygen and other dangers that occur in space.

SUPERNOVA
The name given to an exploding star. This is the largest explosion known to happen in space.

TANK ARMOUR
Super-strong materials used to reinforce vehicles that are used in combat.

VOLUME
The amount of three-dimensional space that an object takes up.

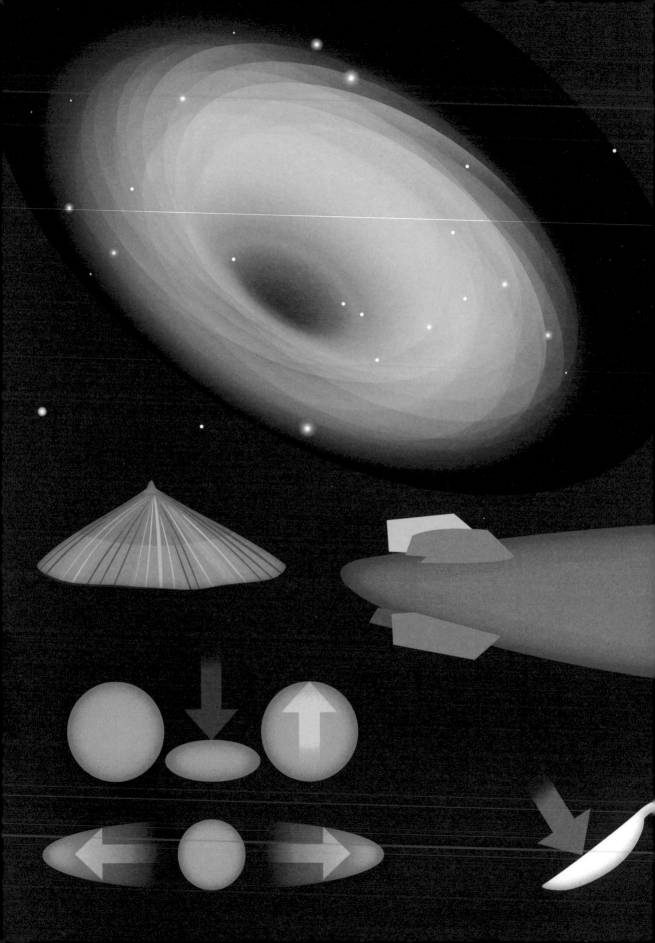